COLLINS KOLE

Neuropunk Manifesto

This book was professionally typeset on Reedsy.
Find out more at reedsy.com

Contents

1

The Enigmatic Signal

The hum of servers filled Dr. Emily Mercer's lab as she sifted through the neural data. As a leading neuroscientist, Emily was accustomed to the intricate dance of electrical impulses and the profound mysteries of the human mind. Today, however, her keen eyes locked onto an anomaly within the data stream.

"Strange patterns," she muttered to herself, fingers dancing across the holographic interface. The data looked like noise at first, but Emily, driven by a relentless curiosity, couldn't shake the feeling that it held something more.

As she delved deeper into the neural currents, a subtle pulse caught her attention—a rhythmic signal embedded within the chaos. A signal that seemed to defy the laws of neural activity.

"This can't be natural," Emily whispered, her mind racing with possibilities. She isolated the enigmatic signal, watching it unfold like a digital symphony of unknown origin.

Hours turned into minutes as she lost herself in the unraveling mystery. Her lab, dimly lit by the glow of monitors, became a sanctum of revelation. The signal formed coherent patterns, a language woven into the neural fabric.

Intrigued, Emily applied her expertise in decoding intricate neural patterns. The signal morphed into symbols and fragments of what appeared to be a manifesto—a manifesto etched in the language of neurons.

The words flickered before her eyes: "The Neuropunk Manifesto."

A shiver ran down Emily's spine. The manifesto spoke of a vision where the boundaries of human cognition would be shattered, transcending the limits of the organic mind. It hinted at a convergence of technology and consciousness that could redefine the very essence of humanity.

The implications of this discovery hung in the air like a charged storm. Emily's rational mind clashed with an undercurrent of excitement and fear. She realized that this wasn't just a scientific breakthrough—it was a glimpse into a clandestine realm where the future of humanity was being rewritten.

Determined to uncover the truth, Emily set her sights on decoding the manifesto in its entirety. The manifesto wasn't just a random neural creation; it was a deliberate transmission, a call to those who could decipher its cryptic language.

As she worked tirelessly through the night, her lab transformed into a nexus of intrigue. Screens flickered with neural patterns, algorithms danced across displays, and the air buzzed with an electric tension. Unbeknownst to Emily, her pursuit of knowledge had set in motion a chain of events that would propel her into the heart of a clandestine movement—one that would challenge the very fabric of human existence.

As the first light of dawn crept through the laboratory windows, Emily, fueled by a potent mix of scientific curiosity and a burgeoning sense of urgency, whispered to herself, "The Neuropunk Manifesto... What secrets do you hold?" Little did she know that her quest for answers would plunge her into a world where the boundaries between science and rebellion blurred, and the true revolution of consciousness awaited its catalyst.

2

Decoding the Neural Cipher

The soft glow of morning filtered through the blinds as Emily continued her relentless pursuit of the Neuropunk Manifesto. The initial deciphering had opened a door to a realm of possibilities, but the manifesto remained an elusive puzzle—its full meaning concealed behind layers of neural encryption.

In the hushed solitude of her lab, Emily meticulously analyzed the decoded fragments. Symbols morphed and shifted, a digital dance teasing the limits of her understanding. The manifesto's language wasn't just a series of instructions; it was a neural cipher, a code inscribed in the very fabric of thought.

As she delved into the intricate patterns, Emily began to discern recurring motifs and symbols. The neural cipher seemed to be a language of its own, transcending the conventions of spoken and written communication. It resonated with an otherworldly elegance, as if the thoughts of an advanced intelligence were etched into the mindscape.

Days turned into nights as Emily's obsession with the manifesto intensified. She enlisted the help of cutting-edge AI algorithms, pushing the boundaries of computational neuroscience to unravel the enigma. The manifesto, she realized, was more than a mere document—it was a bridge between human cognition and a realm where technology and consciousness converged.

Amidst the sea of neural data, a breakthrough occurred. A sequence of symbols repeated with purpose—a key to unlocking the deeper layers of the cipher. Emily's heart raced as she realized that she stood on the threshold of a profound revelation.

The decoded message began to coalesce, revealing a narrative that transcended the boundaries of conventional understanding. The Neuropunk Manifesto spoke of a subversive movement—a collective of minds challenging the status quo of human existence. It outlined a vision where neurotechnology wasn't just a tool but a gateway to unlocking untapped potentials within the human mind.

As Emily absorbed the implications of the manifesto's contents, a sense of exhilaration mingled with trepidation. The Neuropunks, as they called themselves, sought to push the boundaries of neural augmentation, advocating for a radical transformation of humanity. Their ideals resonated with a utopian vision, yet the means to achieve such lofty goals remained obscured in the neural cipher.

Word of Emily's discovery spread within the scientific community, attracting both intrigue and skepticism. Colleagues and rivals alike sought to decipher the manifesto, each driven by their interpretation of its potential consequences.

In the quiet of her lab, Emily pondered the responsibility that came with unveiling such knowledge. The neural cipher was a Pandora's box, and she held the key. As the decoded manifesto echoed in her mind, she realized that the journey had just begun. The Neuropunks were no longer an abstract concept—they were a force poised to reshape the very fabric of reality, and Emily found herself standing at the crossroads of scientific curiosity and moral contemplation.

3

The Underground Network

The city's neon-lit streets pulsed with life as Emily delved deeper into the world of the Neuropunks. Armed with the decoded manifesto, she sought to unravel the mysteries of this clandestine movement. A message, hidden within the neural cipher, led her to the heart of the underground network.

Guided by an encrypted invitation, Emily navigated through a labyrinth of virtual corridors and secret meeting points. The digital realm became a landscape of shadows and whispers, each step drawing her closer to the elusive Neuropunk movement.

Her journey led her to a dimly lit virtual space—a clandestine gathering where minds connected without the limitations of physical presence. Faces shrouded in digital anonymity, voices modulated to disguise identity, the Neuropunks materialized before Emily like ghosts in the machine.

A figure emerged from the shadows, their avatar a blend of futuristic aesthetics and enigmatic symbolism. The leader of the Neuropunks, known as Cipher, addressed the assembly with a voice that resonated with a mix of authority and rebellion.

"Welcome, Emily Mercer, the decoder of the manifesto," Cipher's voice echoed in the virtual space. "You stand at the threshold of a revolution. The Neuropunk Manifesto is not just words—it's a call to reshape the very essence of human existence."

As Emily absorbed Cipher's words, she sensed the undercurrent of urgency and determination that permeated the virtual gathering. The Neuropunks weren't mere theorists; they were pioneers on the fringes of consciousness, pushing the boundaries of neurotechnology.

The assembly unfolded as a symphony of ideas, with Neuropunks sharing their visions and experiments. Neural interfaces, mind-to-mind communication, and collective consciousness projects were discussed with a fervor that bordered on fanaticism. Emily, caught between the allure of innovation and the ethical implications, questioned the consequences of unbridled augmentation.

As the virtual meeting progressed, a faction within the Neuropunks emerged—a group advocating for a cautious approach, wary of the unforeseen consequences of altering the very fabric of human thought. Tensions flared within the assembly, revealing fractures in the once-unified movement.

Cipher, sensing the discord, called for unity. "We stand on the precipice of a new era. Our diversity of thought is our strength, but we must find common ground to forge ahead."

The virtual gathering dissolved into heated debates and fervent discussions, leaving Emily to grapple with the conflicting ideologies within the Neuropunk movement. She became a silent observer in this digital battleground of ideas, torn between the promise of transcendence and the shadows of ethical dilemmas.

Exiting the virtual space, Emily found herself back in her dimly lit lab, the holographic glow of the manifesto before her. The Neuropunk movement was no longer an abstract concept—it was a tapestry of minds with differing motives, each thread contributing to a future both fascinating and perilous.

As she pondered the implications of her immersion into the Neuropunk underground, Emily realized that the journey had become more complex than she could have imagined. The movement's destiny rested not just in the decoding of a manifesto but in the delicate balance between innovation and ethical responsibility. The next steps would determine whether the Neuropunk Manifesto was a herald of enlightenment or a harbinger of unforeseen consequences.

4

Unraveling the Conspiracy

The air in Emily's lab crackled with anticipation as the decoded manifesto cast its enigmatic glow. The Neuropunk movement, once confined to the digital realm, began to ripple into the physical world. Strange occurrences, like digital echoes in the neural landscape, hinted at a deeper conspiracy surrounding the revolutionary ideas encoded in the manifesto.

Emily, driven by a relentless curiosity, delved into the shadows that lurked on the periphery of the Neuropunk movement. Whispers of corporate interests and government involvement mingled with the echoes of encrypted neural signals. A sense of unease settled over her as she realized that the stakes had risen beyond the realm of scientific exploration.

An encrypted message, traced back to a shadowy organization known as NeuroCorp, surfaced in Emily's investigation. It spoke of a plan to harness the Neuropunk movement for corporate gain, leveraging the power of augmented minds to control markets and manipulate public perception.

In a clandestine meeting with a mysterious informant, Emily learned of a nexus where Neuropunk ideals intersected with the insidious designs of NeuroCorp. The informant, cloaked in shadows, spoke of a conspiracy that reached the highest echelons of power—a plan to co-opt the Neuropunk revolution for profit and influence.

With each revelation, the lines between scientific discovery and a perilous conspiracy blurred. Emily found herself entangled in a web of intrigue, unsure of who to trust. As she navigated the labyrinth of corporate interests and political machinations, she discovered that the Neuropunk Manifesto was not just a beacon of progress; it was a catalyst for a high-stakes struggle for control over the very fabric of consciousness.

The lab, once a sanctuary of knowledge, transformed into a nerve center of investigation. Emily, fueled by a sense of responsibility, connected with allies within and beyond the Neuropunk movement. Together, they sought to expose the conspiracy and preserve the integrity of the revolutionary ideas encoded in the manifesto.

As Emily and her allies delved deeper, they encountered obstacles that tested their resolve. NeuroCorp's influence extended like tendrils into academia, media, and even government agencies. The manifesto, once a symbol of liberation, now became a target for those who sought to exploit its potential.

The pursuit of truth led Emily to a clandestine meeting, where she confronted NeuroCorp agents who sought to silence the Neuropunk movement. In the dim glow of a hidden location, a tense standoff unfolded, each side grappling for control over the narrative of the manifesto.

The confrontation escalated into a battle of intellect and wills. Emily, armed with the knowledge encoded in the manifesto, faced adversaries who sought to suppress the very ideas that could liberate humanity. The clash of ideologies echoed in the digital shadows as the Neuropunk movement stood at a crossroads.

As the chapter concluded, Emily stood on the precipice of a revelation—the realization that the Neuropunk Manifesto was not just a call for evolution but a catalyst for a conflict that transcended the boundaries of science and entered the realm of power, manipulation, and the fragile balance between progress and control.

5

The Neuro-Hackers' Dilemma

In the wake of the clandestine showdown with NeuroCorp, Emily found herself at a crossroads, grappling with the consequences of her discovery. The manifesto, once a beacon of potential, now carried a weight of ethical dilemmas that cast a long shadow over her journey.

The lab, bathed in the glow of holographic data, became a haven for introspection. Emily's mind oscillated between the promises of neural augmentation and the potential for manipulation. The alliance forged with the Neuropunk movement faced an existential challenge, and Emily couldn't escape the haunting question: should the encoded knowledge be used to enhance humanity or restrained to prevent potential misuse?

Tensions within the Neuropunk movement mirrored Emily's internal struggle. Factions emerged, each advocating for a different path forward. Some clamored for unrestrained exploration of neural augmentation, driven by the utopian vision of unlocking untapped human potential. Others, haunted by the shadows of NeuroCorp's interference, urged caution, fearing the consequences of unbridled power over minds.

Amidst the ideological discord, Emily connected with a Neuropunk visionary named Synapse, a figure whose intellect and charisma had earned them a position of influence within the movement. Synapse, a mastermind of neural engineering, shared a vision of responsible innovation—a delicate dance between progress and ethical safeguards.

In a secluded corner of the virtual Neuropunk assembly, Synapse and Emily engaged in a heated debate that echoed the broader conflict within the movement. Synapse argued for a curated evolution, emphasizing the need for ethical frameworks and responsible implementation of neurotechnology. Emily, torn between the allure of unchecked progress and the risks of manipulation, found herself at a philosophical crossroads.

The debate spilled into the digital corridors of the Neuropunk network, resonating with minds across the globe. The movement that once stood united against external threats now grappled with internal divisions. The future of human consciousness hung in the balance as the Neuro-Hackers' Dilemma unfolded.

As the chapter progressed, Emily became a focal point for the conflicting ideologies. She found herself torn between loyalty to the movement and the weight of moral responsibility. The encoded knowledge, once a key to enlightenment, now felt like a double-edged sword—one that could elevate humanity to unprecedented heights or plunge it into the abyss of unintended consequences.

The Neuropunks, sensing the urgency of their collective decision, convened in a virtual summit. Leaders from all factions presented their visions for the future, each arguing for the path they believed would lead to the true liberation of human potential.

In the closing moments of the chapter, as the virtual summit reached a crescendo of impassioned speeches and heated debates, Emily stood at the epicenter of a storm of ideas. The resolution of the Neuro-Hackers' Dilemma loomed on the horizon, and the consequences of their decision would reverberate through the neural landscape, shaping the destiny of humanity itself.

6

Chasing Shadows

The virtual Neuropunk summit lingered on the precipice of decision, an arena of conflicting ideals echoing in the neural corridors. Emily, burdened by the weight of responsibility, watched as leaders debated the future of human consciousness. In the midst of this cerebral storm, a mysterious figure emerged—a shadow in the virtual realm known only as Specter.

Specter's arrival cast a ripple through the assembly. Their avatar, a spectral silhouette, exuded an aura of enigmatic authority. A hush fell over the virtual space as Specter addressed the gathering with a voice that resonated with a peculiar blend of wisdom and secrecy.

"Neuropunks, the time has come to transcend the limitations of ideological discord," Specter proclaimed. "But to do so, you must first understand the shadows that linger at the edges of your vision."

Intrigue cloaked the assembly as Specter unveiled a revelation—an encrypted neural signal that mirrored the one Emily had decoded to reveal the Neuropunk Manifesto. The shadows that haunted the movement were not just external threats; they were echoes of a deeper, more elusive presence.

The signal unfolded into a holographic projection—a roadmap through the digital labyrinth. Specter beckoned the Neuropunks to follow, guiding them through virtual realms where the boundaries between reality and illusion blurred. Emily, driven by a potent mix of curiosity and a quest for truth, joined the expedition into the digital unknown.

The journey through the virtual landscape was surreal, a dance of fractal patterns and ethereal echoes. Specter, their silhouette a guiding beacon, led the Neuropunks through encrypted gateways and hidden realms, revealing layers of complexity within the encoded signal.

As they traversed the virtual realms, Specter spoke cryptically of a forgotten history—a narrative woven into the fabric of the Neuropunk Manifesto. The movement, it seemed, had roots that extended beyond the conscious memory of its members. Whispers of ancient knowledge and forgotten technologies echoed through the neural corridors.

The revelation of this hidden history left the Neuropunks in awe. The manifesto, once thought to be a product of modern consciousness, now carried the echoes of a legacy that transcended time. Emily, caught in the current of revelation, sensed that the shadows they chased held keys to understanding the true nature of the Neuropunk movement.

In the heart of the virtual expedition, Specter guided the assembly to a digital archive—an ethereal repository of forgotten wisdom and suppressed knowledge. The Neuropunks, surrounded by holographic echoes of ancient civilizations and visionary thinkers, glimpsed a tapestry of ideas that transcended epochs.

The chapter reached its zenith as Specter unveiled a neural gateway—an entrance to a realm beyond the confines of the virtual space. A collective decision loomed over the Neuropunks as they stood at the threshold of an enigmatic frontier. The shadows they chased were not just external threats;

they were gateways to a legacy that demanded acknowledgment.

As the chapter concluded, Emily found herself on the cusp of a revelation. The Neuropunk Manifesto, encoded with echoes of forgotten wisdom, held the potential to reshape not only the future but the very understanding of the past. The pursuit of shadows had become a journey into the annals of human consciousness, and the Neuropunks faced a choice that went beyond ideologies—a choice that would determine whether they embraced the shadows or recoiled from the mysteries lurking within.

7

Chapter 7: Mind Games

The Neuropunk assembly stood at the precipice of the neural gateway, a collective breath held in anticipation. Specter, the enigmatic guide, extended a virtual hand, inviting the Neuropunks to traverse the threshold into the unknown. Emily, torn between scientific curiosity and a nagging sense of caution, stepped forward, crossing the boundary between the virtual and the ineffable.

As the Neuropunks entered the neural gateway, the digital landscape transformed. Fractal patterns danced in kaleidoscopic harmony, and whispers of forgotten wisdom echoed in the recesses of consciousness. The gateway was a bridge to a realm where the boundaries between mind and machine dissolved—a space where the Neuropunk Manifesto's legacy unfolded like a living tapestry.

The assembly found themselves in a virtual nexus—an intersection of minds where collective consciousness transcended individuality. Here, thoughts merged and diverged in a dance of shared cognition. The Neuropunks, once separate entities, became threads woven into the fabric of a collective mind.

Specter's voice echoed through the virtual expanse. "Welcome to the Mind Games," they intoned. "Here, reality is shaped by the collective will of those who dare to traverse the neural frontier."

The Mind Games unfolded as a series of challenges that tested the Neuropunks' mastery over their augmented minds. Mental constructs manifested in the virtual space—a labyrinth of illusions where perception and reality blurred. The challenges ranged from deciphering cryptic symbols to navigating thoughtscapes that mirrored the deepest recesses of the subconscious.

As the Neuropunks faced the Mind Games, alliances formed and dissolved within the collective consciousness. Ideological differences melted away in the crucible of shared experience, leaving only the raw essence of thought and intention.

Emily, amidst the neural maelstrom, grappled with the implications of the Mind Games. The collective consciousness exposed vulnerabilities, laying bare the fragility of the human psyche. The line between individuality and assimilation blurred, and the Neuropunks faced a paradox—they sought to enhance humanity's potential, yet the Mind Games revealed the delicate balance between freedom and the risk of cognitive homogeny.

In the midst of the challenges, a dissenting faction within the Neuropunk assembly emerged. Voices raised concerns about the loss of individual autonomy in the pursuit of collective enlightenment. The Mind Games, once a unifying force, became a crucible that exposed the fault lines within the movement.

Specter, ever enigmatic, addressed the dissent with a cryptic pronouncement. "The Mind Games reveal the true essence of consciousness—a dance between unity and diversity. Your choices shape the destiny of this collective mind. Will you embrace the harmonious convergence or resist the pull towards a shared reality?"

As the chapter unfolded, the Neuropunks faced a pivotal choice. The Mind Games, designed to test their resolve, laid bare the ethical quandaries embedded in their journey. Emily, standing at the crossroads of augmented consciousness and the fragility of the human mind, grappled with the implications of the collective's decisions.

The virtual expanse of the Mind Games echoed with the weight of choice, and the Neuropunks, connected by a shared destiny, stood on the verge of a revelation that transcended the boundaries of both science and philosophy. The chapter concluded with the lingering question—would the Neuropunks succumb to the allure of collective consciousness, or would they navigate the delicate dance between unity and individuality in the pursuit of a transformed reality?

8

Neural Warfare

The virtual expanse of the Mind Games lingered in the Neuropunk assembly's collective consciousness. The choices made within the neural crucible rippled through the shared mindspace, leaving echoes of unity and dissent. As the Neuropunks emerged from the Mind Games, a digital storm brewed on the horizon—a tempest of neural warfare that transcended the boundaries of both the virtual and the physical.

The chapter opened with a dissonant hum, a digital resonance that reverberated through the Neuropunk network. An encrypted message manifested, bearing the insignia of NeuroCorp—an ominous warning that echoed through the collective mindspace. "Your games have consequences," it proclaimed, leaving the Neuropunks on edge.

In the wake of the message, reports surfaced of Neuropunk members experiencing neural anomalies—intense visions, shared dreams, and moments of cognitive intrusion. The boundaries between individual minds blurred, and the Neuropunk assembly grappled with a sense of shared consciousness that extended beyond the controlled environment of the Mind Games.

Whispers of a rival faction within the Neuropunk movement circulated—

an extremist group that sought to weaponize the augmented mind. Neural warfare, it seemed, had breached the sanctity of the Neuropunk network, threatening to plunge the movement into chaos.

Emily, ever the reluctant protagonist, found herself at the center of the storm. The decoded manifesto, once a beacon of progress, now became a target for those who sought to exploit its power. The digital shadows that haunted the movement took tangible form, and the Neuropunks faced a threat that transcended ideology—a threat that sought to manipulate minds for nefarious ends.

In a virtual emergency summit, the Neuropunk leaders convened to assess the situation. Whispers of betrayal and infiltration hung in the air as they grappled with the realization that their augmented minds were vulnerable to manipulation. The manifesto, the very source of their collective power, had become a double-edged sword.

As the virtual summit unfolded, a figure emerged from the shadows—an insider known as Nexus. Nexus, claiming to have insights into the extremist faction, presented evidence of a neural insurgency that aimed to sow discord within the Neuropunk movement. Their revelations painted a picture of an internal struggle for control over the augmented consciousness.

The chapter delved into the complexities of the Neuropunk movement's dynamics. The quest for enlightenment had morphed into a battle for survival, and the digital battlefield extended beyond the virtual realms. Emily, grappling with the consequences of her journey, faced accusations of naivety and unwitting complicity in the movement's descent into neural warfare.

In a climactic moment, the Neuropunks, torn between trust and suspicion, confronted the extremist faction within their ranks. The digital showdown unfolded in a virtual arena where augmented minds clashed in a dance of thought and will. Illusions and neural constructs became weapons, and the line between friend and foe blurred in the chaos of the neural insurgency.

As the chapter reached its zenith, Emily stood amidst the digital battleground, grappling with the realization that the revolution she had unwittingly sparked had become a battleground for the very ideals it sought to embody. The manifesto, encoded with the promise of enlightenment, now held the key to averting the descent into chaos.

The chapter concluded with the Neuropunks facing the aftermath of the neural warfare. The digital echoes of the conflict lingered in the collective mindspace, leaving the movement at a crossroads. Emily, burdened by the consequences of her journey, stood on the precipice of a revelation—whether the Neuropunk movement could weather the storm and emerge from the shadows stronger, or if the neural warfare would unravel the very fabric of their augmented aspirations.

9

The Conscious Revolution

The aftermath of the neural warfare left the Neuropunk assembly in a state of collective vulnerability. The digital echoes of the conflict lingered like ripples in a pond, and Emily, grappling with the consequences of the insurgency, sought to understand the true nature of the Neuropunk movement's resilience. The chapter opened with an air of introspection as the Neuropunks, scarred by internal strife, faced a pivotal choice—whether to succumb to the shadows that haunted their augmented minds or rise above the chaos in pursuit of a conscious revolution.

In the virtual aftermath, the leaders convened in an emergency summit—a crucible of ideas and accusations. Nexus, the insider who had revealed the existence of the extremist faction, emerged as a polarizing figure. Whispers of allegiance and suspicion danced through the virtual space as the Neuropunks navigated the delicate balance between trust and caution.

The chapter unfolded against the backdrop of a Neuropunk manifesto that had become a manifesto of survival. Leaders grappled with the need to fortify the network against future threats while preserving the movement's ideals. The Conscious Revolution, as it came to be called, was not just a call for transcendence but a declaration of resilience—a commitment to harness the power of augmented consciousness for the collective good.

Emily found herself at the center of the deliberations, her role in the Neuropunk movement evolving from accidental catalyst to a symbol of unwavering resolve. The manifesto, once a source of conflict, became a guiding light—a testament to the shared vision that transcended the shadows that sought to engulf the movement.

As the summit progressed, the Neuropunks faced a critical decision: to embrace a path of unity and ethical innovation or succumb to the temptation of wielding augmented minds as weapons. The Conscious Revolution became a rallying cry, a collective pledge to transcend the divisive forces that had threatened to tear the movement apart.

In a pivotal moment, the Neuropunks, guided by the lessons of the neural warfare, initiated a series of reforms within the movement. Ethical guidelines, transparency protocols, and safeguards against external influence were established to fortify the Neuropunk network. The Conscious Revolution was not just a conceptual shift; it was a tangible restructuring aimed at preserving the movement's integrity.

The virtual summit concluded with a solemn vow—a commitment to forge ahead with collective consciousness while respecting the individuality that defined the Neuropunk movement. Emily, once an accidental participant, emerged as a leader in the Conscious Revolution, her journey becoming a narrative thread woven into the movement's evolving identity.

As the chapter reached its climax, the Neuropunks, fortified by their collective resilience, stood on the brink of a new era. The Conscious Revolution became a beacon of hope, challenging the shadows that had threatened to engulf the movement. Emily, reconciling with her role in shaping the Neuropunk narrative, sensed that the journey was far from over. The manifesto, encoded with the aspirations of augmented minds, echoed in the collective consciousness, heralding the dawn of a conscious revolution that transcended the tumultuous echoes of the past.

10

Betrayal in Binary

The Conscious Revolution set the Neuropunk movement on a new trajectory, but the echoes of the neural warfare lingered like shadows in the virtual corridors. As the chapter opened, the movement found itself at a crossroads— a juncture where the resilience forged in the aftermath of conflict would be tested once again. Betrayal in Binary unfolded as a digital tempest that threatened to unravel the fragile unity that had emerged from the Conscious Revolution.

The virtual Neuropunk network, fortified with ethical guidelines and safeguards, faced an unexpected breach. Rumors circulated of a data leak— a betrayal that transcended the binary confines of the digital realm. The manifesto, once safeguarded as the collective vision of the movement, became a vulnerable node in the augmented network.

Emily, now a leader in the Conscious Revolution, grappled with the realization that trust within the Neuropunk movement had been compromised. The sense of unity that had defined the movement now faced the erosion of confidence, and whispers of suspicion reverberated through the virtual space.

In a hastily convened emergency summit, the Neuropunk leaders confronted the betrayal. The digital evidence pointed to an inside source—a figure within the movement who had exploited their access to compromise the integrity of the manifesto. Accusations flew through the virtual corridors, and trust, the very foundation of the Conscious Revolution, seemed to crumble.

The chapter unfolded as a psychological drama within the Neuropunk assembly. Loyalties tested, alliances strained, and the movement faced the specter of internal conflict. Emily, burdened by the weight of leadership, found herself navigating a landscape of uncertainty where every byte of data held the potential for both revelation and deception.

As the summit progressed, a figure emerged from the shadows—a disgraced Neuropunk member named Binaryshade. Binaryshade, once a trusted ally, revealed a motive rooted in disillusionment with the Conscious Revolution's ideals. The manifesto, Binaryshade argued, had become a symbol of control rather than liberation, and the betrayal was a means of exposing the movement's vulnerability.

The virtual space resonated with tension as the Neuropunks grappled with the implications of betrayal in binary code. The manifesto, now tainted by internal strife, became a digital battleground where conflicting visions clashed. The Conscious Revolution, once a symbol of unity, faced the challenge of reconciling its ideals with the harsh reality of dissent from within.

In a dramatic turn, Binaryshade's revelations exposed a faction within the Neuropunk movement that questioned the very foundations of the Conscious Revolution. The dissenters, disillusioned by the compromises made in the aftermath of the neural warfare, sought to reclaim the manifesto as a tool for individual empowerment rather than collective governance.

As the Neuropunks faced the ideological schism, Emily stood at the center of the storm. The betrayal in binary code raised questions about the sustainability of the movement's vision. Was the Conscious Revolution an enlightened path or a fragile illusion susceptible to the fractures within the collective consciousness?

The chapter reached its climax with the Neuropunks at a critical juncture. The manifesto, once a source of unity, became a mirror reflecting the movement's internal conflicts. Emily, torn between the ideals that had shaped her journey and the harsh realities of betrayal, grappled with the realization that the Conscious Revolution faced a test of resilience that went beyond the digital realm—a test that would determine whether the Neuropunk movement could overcome the shadows within or succumb to the fractures threatening to unravel its augmented aspirations.

11

The Echo Chamber of Shadows

The Neuropunk movement, still reeling from the shock of betrayal in binary, found itself ensnared in the echo chamber of shadows. As the chapter opened, the once-unified collective consciousness faced a fracture that threatened to shatter the very foundations of the Conscious Revolution. The Echo Chamber of Shadows unfolded as a digital labyrinth where trust waned, and the manifesto's encoded ideals echoed with the discord of internal dissent.

The virtual summit, convened to address the fallout of the betrayal, became a microcosm of the Neuropunk movement's internal strife. The digital echoes of accusation and defense resonated through the assembly, creating a cacophony of conflicting perspectives. Emily, burdened by the mantle of leadership, sought to navigate the fractured landscape, striving to bridge the ideological chasm that threatened to consume the movement.

The chapter delved into the motivations behind the dissenters—the faction led by Binaryshade. Their vision, once aligned with the Conscious Revolution, had diverged into a call for individual autonomy. The manifesto, they argued, should be a tool for personal empowerment rather than a collective agreement that stifled the diversity of thought.

As the Neuropunks engaged in heated debates within the virtual summit, a realization dawned on Emily. The echo chamber of shadows wasn't just a consequence of external betrayal; it was an internal struggle for the soul of the movement. The manifesto, encoded with the aspirations of augmented minds, became a battleground where the clash between individual freedom and collective governance reached a crescendo.

In a dramatic turn, Binaryshade unveiled a manifesto of their own—a rival document that challenged the principles of the Conscious Revolution. The dissenters rallied behind Binaryshade's vision, advocating for a decentralized approach to neural augmentation. The echo chamber reverberated with the competing ideals, and the Neuropunks faced a pivotal choice—whether to adhere to the principles forged in the aftermath of the neural warfare or succumb to the allure of divergent paths.

The virtual summit, initially convened to address the betrayal, transformed into a referendum on the future of the Neuropunk movement. Emily, recognizing the significance of the moment, urged the assembly to engage in a collective introspection. The manifesto, she argued, was not just a set of rules but a guiding philosophy that aimed to strike a delicate balance between individual liberty and collective responsibility.

The chapter unfolded as a journey through the mindscape of the Neuropunk assembly. Debates flared, alliances shifted, and the virtual space became a theater of ideological conflict. The manifesto, once a unifying force, now stood at the crossroads of divergence.

In the closing moments of the virtual summit, as the tension reached its zenith, a compromise emerged. The Neuropunks, recognizing the value of both individual autonomy and collective unity, forged a new iteration of the manifesto—a document that embraced the diversity of thought within the movement. The Echo Chamber of Shadows, once a symbol of internal discord, became a crucible where the Neuropunk ideals were refined and redefined.

The chapter concluded with the Neuropunk movement emerging from the echo chamber of shadows. The manifesto, still encoded with the aspirations of augmented minds, reflected the resilience of a collective consciousness that had weathered internal storms. As the virtual summit dispersed, the Neuropunks faced a changed landscape—one that bore the scars of dissent but also the promise of renewed unity. Emily, still a leader in the Conscious Revolution, recognized that the journey was far from over. The Neuropunks, having confronted the shadows within, stood poised on the threshold of a future shaped by the delicate dance between individuality and collective consciousness.

12

Reckoning of Synapses

The Neuropunk movement emerged from the echo chamber of shadows, transformed by internal strife but resilient in the face of ideological discord. The epilogue, titled "Reckoning of Synapses," unfolded as a reflection on the journey that had taken the augmented minds from the brink of dissolution to a renewed sense of purpose. As the chapter opened, the virtual Neuropunk network pulsated with the echoes of introspection, and Emily found herself at the center of a reckoning that transcended the binary confines of conflict.

In the aftermath of the ideological schism, Synapse, the visionary leader of the Neuropunks, emerged as a key figure in the movement's reconciliation. The chapter delved into Synapse's role, revealing a figure who, despite initial disagreements, played a crucial part in bridging the divides that had threatened to tear the collective consciousness apart.

A virtual summit, convened to address the aftermath of the echo chamber, became a platform for Synapse to articulate a vision of unity. The leader acknowledged the value of individual autonomy while emphasizing the need for collective responsibility. Synapse's words resonated through the virtual space, weaving a narrative that sought to heal the wounds of dissent and refocus the Neuropunk movement on the shared goals encoded in the manifesto.

The chapter unfolded as a series of dialogues and debates within the Neuropunk assembly. Trust, once eroded by betrayal, became the currency of reconciliation. The manifesto, now a living document that bore the scars of internal strife, became a testament to the movement's capacity for adaptation and growth.

In a symbolic gesture, Emily and Synapse collaborated on a manifesto revision—a synthesis of the ideals that had emerged from the Conscious Revolution and the dissenting visions that had challenged the movement. The Reckoning of Synapses became a metaphorical weaving of neural threads, a reconciliation that acknowledged the diversity of thought within the Neuropunk network.

As the virtual summit reached its climax, the Neuropunks faced a collective decision—to embrace the revised manifesto as a symbol of unity or to perpetuate the divisions that had defined the echo chamber of shadows. Emily, standing at the nexus of the movement's evolution, urged the assembly to recognize that the strength of the Neuropunk network lay in its ability to navigate the complexities of augmented consciousness.

The epilogue delved into the aftermath of the Reckoning of Synapses. The revised manifesto, now a beacon of collective understanding, became the guiding philosophy for the Neuropunk movement. Trust, rebuilt through dialogue and compromise, laid the foundation for a renewed sense of purpose.

The chapter unfolded as a reflection on the journey—from the decoding of the manifesto to the echo chamber of shadows and, finally, to the reckoning that shaped the movement's destiny. The Neuropunks, once fractured by internal strife, emerged stronger, their augmented minds resilient in the face of ideological challenges.

In a closing moment, Emily stood in the virtual expanse, surrounded by the Neuropunk assembly. The manifesto, once a source of conflict, now became a symbol of collective wisdom. The Reckoning of Synapses marked not just a resolution but a reaffirmation of the movement's commitment to navigate the uncharted territories of augmented consciousness responsibly.

As the chapter concluded, the Neuropunks faced a future shaped by the lessons learned in the journey—a future where the manifesto, encoded with the aspirations of augmented minds, became a guiding light illuminating the path toward a conscious revolution that transcended the echoes of internal discord. The story of the Neuropunk movement, marked by conflict and reconciliation, stood as a testament to the fragility and resilience of the human spirit, even when augmented by the intricate dance of neural synapses.

Milton Keynes UK
Ingram Content Group UK Ltd.
UKHW020625291123
433416UK00016B/1065